WonderWorks

Decodable Reader

Unit 1

McGraw Hill

Contents

I Can
by Margaret Nelson
illustrated by Angela Adams
1

Can I?
by Neela Gupta
illustrated by Kersti Frigell
9

We Can
by Claude Martin
illustrated by Kersti Frigell
17

I Can

by Margaret Nelson
illustrated by Angela Adams

I can  .

hear

I can  see .

I can  .

smile

I **can**  .

smell

I can  .

taste

I can  .

hug

Can I?

by Neela Gupta
illustrated by Kersti Frigell

I can  pack **the**  lunchbox.

I can  pack **the**  napkin.

I can  **the** 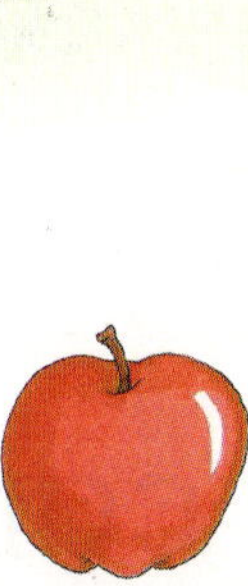 .

pack apple

I can  the  .

pack egg

I can  pack **the**  sandwich.

Can I  eat **the**  lunch ?

We Can

by Claude Martin

illustrated by Kersti Frigell

We can 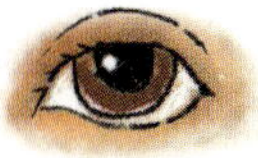 see the  trees.

We can  the  .

see children

We can 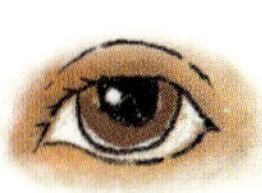 the  .

see swings

We can 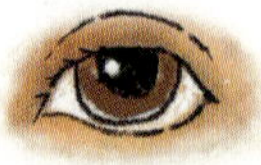 see the  slide.

We can  the  .

see sandbox

We can 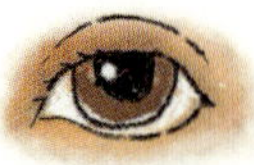 the  .

see park

Unit 1

Decoding skills taught to date:

Consonant /m/*m*, Short *a*